No More Paycheck to Paycheck

Get out of the Rat Race and Start Living a Fulfilling Life!

Frank Carlson

Copyright © dsk-enterprise Inc Ltd., 2020

All rights reserved. No part of this publication may be reproduced in any form without written consent of the author and the publisher. The information contained in this book may not be stored in a retrieval system, or transmitted in any form by any means, electronic, mechanical, photocopying or otherwise without the written consent of the publisher. This book may not be resold, hired out or otherwise disposed by way of trade in any form of binding or cover other than that in which it is published, without the written consent of the publisher. Respective authors own all copyrights not held by the publisher. The presentation of the information is without contract or any type of guarantee assurance. All trademarks and brands within this book are for clarifying purposes only and are the owned by the owners themselves, not affiliated with this document.

Disclaimer

This document is geared towards providing exact and reliable information in regards to the topic and issue covered. The publication is sold with the idea that the publisher is not required to render accounting, officially permitted, or otherwise, qualified services. If advice is necessary, legal or professional, a practiced individual in the profession should be ordered. In no way is it legal to reproduce, duplicate, or transmit any part of this document in either electronic means or in printed format. Recording of this publication is strictly prohibited and any storage of this document is not allowed unless with written permission from the publisher. All rights reserved. The information provided herein is stated to be truthful and consistent, in that any liability, in terms of inattention or otherwise, by any usage or abuse of any policies, processes, or directions contained within is the solitary and utter responsibility of the recipient reader. Under no circumstances will any legal responsibility or blame be held against the publisher for any reparation, damages, or monetary loss due to the information herein, either directly or indirectly. The information herein is offered for informational purposes solely, and is universal as so. The presentation of the information is without contract or any type of guarantee assurance.

This book is not intended for use as a source of legal, medical, business, accounting or financial advice. All readers are advised to seek services of competent professionals in the legal, medical, business, accounting, and finance fields.

Introduction

There are millions of people who get up early every morning to go to a job that they don't like just so they can get a paycheck at the end of the week. If you want to stop living from paycheck to paycheck then you are going to have a new way of thinking.

People who are rich don't need to live from paycheck to paycheck because they always have more than enough money to live off. Rich people pay less in taxes, because of the way they legally structure their finances, so they can accumulate wealth faster. Most importantly rich people don't work for money, they have money working for them. If you are still working for money then you are still living paycheck to paycheck and you need to become financially free.

Table of Contents

1. Why You Should Not Live Paycheck to Paycheck
2. Get Out of the Paycheck to Paycheck Trap
3. Easy Ways to Supplement Your Job Income Online
4. Stop Living Paycheck to Paycheck
5. 10 Ways to Save Money to Buy a House If You Are Living Paycheck to Paycheck
6. It is Time For a Change - Financial Freedom is Not Just a Dream
7. Paycheck to Paycheck Paramedic Method
8. 12 Secrets To Reduce Your Debt And Stop Living From Paycheck To Paycheck
9. 60% of Americans Living Paycheck to Paycheck
10. Paycheck Advances Online: A Much Needed Service

Chapter I

Why You Should Not Live Paycheck to Paycheck

Let me ask you a simple question. Do you have to wait to get paid to pay your bills each month? If you're like most people, you probably do. What would happen if for some reason you lost your job tomorrow? What would be the first bill that would go unpaid? Electricity, cable, food, insurance, possibly phone service? It's a tough decision to make and it gets tougher the longer it takes for you to find a new paycheck. This is the reason you should not live paycheck to paycheck!

Imagine being able to pay your bills comfortably each month with money you already have saved up. Your bill comes in the mail and you immediately pay it. You no longer have to put it in a pile on the counter until you are able to get your next paycheck. How great would that be?

If you have been struggling with money issues, this probably sounds like some made up scenario. However, quite the opposite is true. Many people do not live paycheck to paycheck. These aren't rich and wealthy people I am talking about. These people are just like you and have figured out how to remove the stress of paying their monthly bills from their lives.

It's not as hard as it may seem. Of course it will take some sacrifice on your part to get started, but isn't it worth it to remove some of your financial headaches. You know the headaches you get when you can't pay your bills on time or you receive that ridiculous overdraft or late fee.

Moving Beyond Paycheck to Paycheck Living

According to a 2006 survey released by the American Payroll Association, an estimated 65 percent of Americans live paycheck to paycheck. What's even more frightening than the idea that two-thirds of us are barely getting by is the fact that the findings were fairly universal across income levels. This means that the four-person family living off of $35,000 per year and the young, twenty-something single making $80,000 are functioning at equal levels of difficulty to just pay the bills.

Although what they're spending the money on obviously plays a role in how fiscally responsible each person is, it ultimately doesn't matter what they're buying - it's what they're not buying that's really important. The longer people go without creating an investment portfolio or retirement plan, the less likely they are to find room in their budget to make one five, ten, or even twenty years from now. In an age when Social Security is struggling and on its way out, this means trouble ahead not only for individuals, but for the economy as a whole.

First Steps

Any good budget starts with cutting back on the non-essentials. Overall, this is the least-heeded advice in the world of finance, because few of us want to stop drinking that morning latte. The good news is, you don't have to.

Instead of looking at ways to pinch pennies, look at ways to pinch dollars, tens of dollars, and hundreds of dollars. It's the larger monthly expenses - the mortgage, the car payment, and the cable bill - that make the biggest impact on the amount of extra cash that could be used for investments. When you create a budget for your lifestyle, factor in long-term investments first, and house payments and other essentials second. This way, you live your life around an income that takes the future into account.

Moving Forward

Saving money is only a drop in the bucket of necessary financial planning. While having a structured budget will go a long way in preparing you to move beyond the paycheck-to-paycheck lifestyle, you also have to implement financial plans that will not only give you a savings "cushion" for daily expenses, but also provide something for the future.

The best way to do this is to hire a financial advisor or investment firm that works with all types of fiscal opportunities. A broker is likely to only look at getting your money on the stock market; a financial advisor is more like a life coach, helping you to devise a plan for your unique fiscal situation, your goals for the future, and even your more immediate goals (such as setting aside a down payment for that first home).

Only by focusing on the "bigger picture," which includes finding a way to make you more financially responsible for the present as well as the future, can you begin to move away from the paycheck-to-paycheck trap and really start looking at how financial investments can benefit you.

Chapter II

Get Out of the Paycheck to Paycheck Trap

Different studies have shown that one-half to two-thirds of people are living paycheck-to-paycheck. That is a pretty alarming statistic! This can be explained in part by the results of the current economy, our own attitudes about money, and the lack of adaption to a changing world.

Change Your Attitude

The place to begin is with your mindset. Regarding paycheck-to-paycheck living, you may well think that "it's just the way things are" or "everybody's doing it", both of which are untrue. Keeping these attitudes will ensure that you will never improve your situation.

Take a little time to think about what got you into your current situation. In an article from Celebrating Financial Freedom entitled "4 Steps to Escape the Paycheck to Paycheck Life for Good", the author identifies the following damaging mind and behavior impediments to financial health.

- You Have Concluded That Debt Is Just A Part of Life - Contrary to what some may think, you do not have to be in debt to survive in today's world. You must decide to make paying off your liabilities your number one priority!
- Luxuries Have Turned Into Needs - Certain luxuries like cable TV, an expensive car, and eating out often have evolved from extras into necessities. These extras will bleed your budget.
- You Are Not Earning Enough - You might be underemployed and making too little effort to maximize your work situation.

- You Are Overspending - You also might be spending more than you make, a common trap for some people. This needs to be controlled.
- You Have No Plan - Basically, you spend your money until it is depleted having no idea where it goes. You really need a plan.
- Money Is So Easy To Spend - Those credit cards feel so easy to swipe and sign---it doesn't quite feel like cash. Yet it is, and then comes the interest.
- You Have A Spending Problem - You have no self-control when it comes to spending, and you may even be a shop-a-holic.
- The Job Market Has Changed - Certainly, the job market has changed, and continues to change. You must learn how to deal with those changes. On this topic, the author recommends a book by Dan Miller entitled "48 Days to the Work

You Love - Preparing for the New Normal."

With some increased awareness of how you got to be where you are, are you now ready to begin your journey to financial health? Here are some specific steps to take along with some helpful links.

Get Out Of Debt

You must come to the realization that debt is a choice. Interest and fees will drain away the money you have earned. Eliminating your debt is the best place to start to reverse your situation.

Here are some areas in which you can save money.

1) Food - Reduce the number of times you eat at restaurants. Pick up some healthy ingredients at a market and make your lunch. This can result in major savings for you. Some more food savings tips for you. Use coupons.

2) Car - Another expensive spending category. If you are able, unload your car payment. Maybe even trade down to a used automobile. Other ways to reduce care expenses are: change oil less frequently, sign up with Automobile Club for roadside assistance, research repair costs, and delay trading in your car. Consider carpooling to work. Assess your car insurance needs. If you have an older car that's paid for, consider doing without collision and comprehensive insurance. Maintain a clean driving record, and be aware of low-mileage discounts, multi-lining with other types of insurance, and group automobile insurance plans from employers, professional, alumni, and other groups.

3) Entertainment - Consider getting rid of your cable TV for Netflix or Hulu. Here are some fun things to do for free. Go to the library for books and DVDs. Take advantage of free music and museums.

4) Clothes - You do not need fancy clothes if you are in debt, Shop with sales, go to thrift stores and discount racks, buy second hand, request clothes for gifts, take care of the clothes you have, and sell clothes you no longer wear.

5) Eliminate Credit Card Debt - Start by calling your credit card companies to see if they will lower your interest rate. The average interest rate for credit cards is around 15 percent but some can go as high as 30 percent. A study was conducted in 2002 which found that half of the participants who requested a lower interest rate were given one. Consider transferring that debt to a lower interest account or arranging a loan to consolidate your debt. If these options are not feasible, prioritize your debts so that you pay off the ones with the highest interest rates first.

6) Medical Debt - You can start by offering to pay cash, if you have it, while still at the

hospital or doctor's office. This can save you 5, 10, or 25 percent right off the top. If you end up paying more than the total bill, you will get a refund. If less, you will be responsible for the rest. When you get a bill in the mail: The portion of your bill which says you "may (not will) owe", can be negotiated. Compare what the bill says your insurance didn't cover with what your insurer's policy states that they do cover. If there is a discrepancy, call the doctor's office to have it remedied. Your provider can also put your bill on hold for 30 to 60 days to avoid it going to a collection agency. Notify your provider about any secondary insurance you may possess. If you already have medical debt, ask about any partial forgiveness programs or request a payment plan with 0 percent interest. Sometimes you can obtain a repayment plan for a year or longer.

7) Student Loans - There is a Public Service Loan Forgiveness Program which can permit those in the military, teachers, non-profits, or public service jobs to have their loans forgiven completely. There are other programs such as Income-Based Repayment which will allow you to pay less than your regular payment if you don't earn enough income. If you want to pay off your balance more quickly, begin bi-weekly payments.

8) Mortgage and IRS Debt - Reduce your mortgage debt with bi-weekly payments. For IRS debt, try arranging an installment plan with them.

In an article entitled "The #1 Way to Stop Living Paycheck to Paycheck" by Alex Thomas Sadler, she offers three useful applications for getting out of debt. They are Pay Off Debt, Ready For Zero, and DebtTracker Pro.

Increase Your Income

Even with cutting your expenses as much as you possibly can, you still may not be able to cover everything. You now need to shift your focus to earning more money. Think about improving your present situation and income at your current job, getting a part-time job or side job, or some combination of these. Take some work-related classes and possibly earn a certificate to boost your income. Your job will often reimburse you for tuition and books. Some other ideas for you: you can do freelance work (and that does not include just writing), become a virtual assistant, bookkeeping, designing, and more. You might enjoy tutoring a subject you enjoy. Sell items you don't need on eBay and Craigslist. Some more money making ideas for you.

Prepare And Stick To A Monthly Budget

By preparing a monthly budget, you can track where the money comes in and goes out. Begin by examining your expenses for the previous month for necessary items like your mortgage or rent, car insurance, groceries, gasoline, etc. Then figure out how much you want to spend each month. Post that number somewhere, pay in cash whenever you can and even consider initiating automatic deposits from your paycheck that will go directly to decreasing your debt. Do this so that you will not be tempted to buy unnecessary luxury items.

Here are five applications that can assist you creating a budget and tracking your spending/savings goals.

- Level Money keeps track of your spending and gives you a sense of how you're doing. It is free and will probably work best for those who have relatively simple and linear financial lives.
- Mint is a very popular app that helps you create a budget and then tracks your spending, monitors your credit score and keeps up with potential

fraud by automatically downloading transactions from bank, credit card and investment accounts. The service allows you to combine all of your finances in one place -- giving you a constant overview of your financial status. You can also set up alerts and automatic bill-pay.

- Budget Boss is a highly visual app that uses graphs and charts to track your budget and goals. It also estimates your future account balances, depending on your current spending habits.
- HomeBudget (iPhone only) is an app that lets you manage account balances, budgets, and bills. You can set up credit and debit accounts and track balances, and it syncs data with other iPhone users and can export to a desktop. Users can take a picture of the receipt and associate it with a "family sync" feature that allows members of the household to

exchange information and work together within a single budget.
- Wally is a tool that shows you what comes in, what goes out, what you have saved and what you have budgeted. Wally helps you get a better understanding of where exactly your money is going, and then helps you set up, as well as track and achieve, various financial goals.

Make A Plan

In addition to budgeting, come up with a plan on a more macro level on how you can stop living paycheck-to-paycheck. Figure out what your big priorities are for both your near and long-term future. These might include buying a house or a car, taking a big vacation, creating an emergency savings fund, or saving for retirement. Remember that paying off debts will improve your credit score for those bigger purchases. Stop wasting money on the little things you don't need so you can acquire the bigger things you do need later on. Make your goals realistic so you won't be discouraged. Spend time with similar people, people with responsible prudent mindsets---spenders can drag you down. Finally, celebrate your successes in eliminating your debt!

Chapter III

Easy Ways to Supplement Your Job Income Online

Hardly a day passes before we read in the newspapers or see on TV the grim reports of a weakening world economy and imminent layoffs. No job is safe and more people are uncertain about their future and their ability to retire comfortably. This has led to spike in stress-related illnesses as people try to cope with their current financial situation. But there is a select few people who have it made. These may or may not be in the regular workforce but they have discovered tactics that easily bring them over $1000 extra dollars in their paycheck every single month. Wouldn't you be grateful if thicameras was you? Well, you too can make this your reality if you follow very simply proven steps.

What on Earth Do These People Do?

About 80% of the workforce is consists of workers who probably live from paycheck to paycheck. While this could easily be done a decade ago, it is a risky place to find oneself in these times we are in. Living paycheck to paycheck can be disastrous in the event that your job is eliminated. Job cuts are the order of the day and even very stable companies are doing it. This essentially means no one is safe and the sooner you begin to think about supplementing your income, the better.

Then there is the 20% who whether there is a recession or not they have it made. This is because they had anticipated the downturn in the economy and had braced themselves. This bunch of people have made the necessary moves to secure an autopilot secure income while the rest of the 80% worries about whether their jobs will be there tomorrow or not.

It's All In The Mind

What keeps people as talented as you are on their current treadmill of living paycheck to paycheck? Is it a lack of confidence possibly? It's all in the mind. When you start believing that you too can succeed in supplementing your income in a recession, you will. Recessions are simply opportunities and those that succeed in these times are those that believe that.

Invest In Knowledge

You cannot get where you want to go unless you listen and learn from those that have gone ahead of you. These are people such as myself who have coached many in this journey of supplementing your income. Before you go any further, make a determination to learn something new today. Make a small investment in yourself. This will pay off handsomely. Whether its a book on Amazon or an e-book, it is wise to make that move and catch some knowledge. This is what separates that real success stories from the wannabes.

Chapter IV

Stop Living Paycheck to Paycheck

It's easy in times of a economic recession to get stuck living paycheck to paycheck without the possibility of getting ahead. You cannot afford to switch jobs, start business ventures, and the fear of getting laid off increases because many barely are making enough to get by.

I have been in this situation before, and I have witnessed my parents go through this situation most of my childhood. These situations of worry and doubt leave no room for prosperity or hope. You must find ways to reduce your expenses, live in a cheaper apartment, and cut cost where available. Do not focus on living with less, make the cuts needed, but see that as a step to future growth and happiness. Your current cuts will make your future life more abundant.

Take Responsibility

Wherever you are right now, you are there for a reason. Dwelling on those reasons will not bring you success. You must accept what has happened in the past and view mistakes and downfalls as learning experiences. The only person or thing that can currently change your financial future and happiness is you! The title for this blog is success demands action, will you accept responsibility for yourself and take the action required? If not, you can exit this blog now, and continue to live the life you are living, God bless and best wishes.

Now for the people that are willing to take responsibility, congratulations. Your success is now just a matter of time. Take control of your current situation, stop procrastinating, and look forward to your bright and happy future. The only way your current situation will change, is if you take one hundred percent responsibility and take the actions necessary.

Pay Yourself First

I purchased the audio book The Richest Man In Babylon by George Clason a few years ago, and the main principle conveyed is that you must pay yourself first. Many people pay their bills first instead of themselves. You must begin to budget your money, and set aside a certain percentage weekly of your total amount earned towards savings and future investments.

I set aside ten percent of my weekly amount earned. Budget your money and figure out how much you can set aside as well, and make it a priority to always set aside that percentage first, before you pay any bills. A good way to get into this habit is to make it automated, set up a savings account and have the percentage taken out weekly from your check. If the money is out of sight, its out of mind, you will never miss it.

The key to this system is not spending this money, save this money only for investments. You must make your money make you more money. After you have a significant amount in savings, look for opportunities in which you can invest. If you are not sure what to invest in, you can always take some of your money and throw it into bonds and Cd's. Make sure you are smart about whatever you invest in. Don't take advice from people who are not making money from what they are suggesting. Investing is not risky, as long as your smart. Time is money, and the longer your money is sitting there not making you more money, you are losing money. Start to find ways to invest as you begin to build your savings.

Decide You Deserve Better

People generally earn, what they deserve they should earn. The main reason you are not earning more is because you do not believe you should be earning more. Stop thinking that, you have taken responsibility for your actions and you have committed yourself to taking action. You must begin to realize that what you think is what you get, if you believe you deserve more, you will get more. It's as simple as that.

Take whatever you are earning right now and multiply it by whatever reasonable amount you feel you should. How's your future income feel? Take a moment to visualize it, what would you do with this increased income? How would you be living? How would you feel? What would you be doing? Make this amount a statement and write it down somewhere where you will see it daily. Make it similar to; I will be receiving blank weekly by certain date because I have taken responsibility and I will take the action necessary to receive this goal.
Definiteness is important because it holds

yourself accountable, do not let yourself procrastinate!

6 Ways to Stop Living Paycheck to Paycheck

If you are one of many who find there is too much month and not enough paycheck, if you are slammed month after month with over-draft fee because you did not check your bank account balance before payday, then maybe it is time to make some changes. Before swearing off restaurants or cutting up your credit cards, read the following 8 solutions, which will help get you back on top of your finances.

Know where you spend your money. Failing to track your spending is a sure way to get caught off guard. Most people give a cursory look at their credit card statements, some check their other bills for errors, few bother to really track how their money. This suggests you probably do not recognize when you are spending more on groceries, or your power bill is higher than normal. There are several online financial management tools you can use to track your spending - my favorite is mint.com. Not only is the service free, it will automatically link to your accounts and let you track them all from one page.

Focus on the long term. People who create short time frame budgets are more likely to get off track and lose sight of their long term goals and needs. Weekly or monthly budgeters tend to neglect unforeseen expenses, car repairs, gifts, and emergencies. The result is you underestimate your spending and come up short. People who budget longer term, such as by the year, are more likely to plan for these expenses.

Identify the leaks. Knowing where your money goes will help you identify areas you spend money that have less expensive or free alternatives; a cab ride when you could walk, a restaurant lunch when you could pack leftovers, purchasing a DVD when you could rent from red box for a buck. It is usually the small, daily or weekly nickel and dime expenses that just slip through your fingers and add up. Before you realize it you could be out more than a $100. Depending on your job an office outing for lunch may be necessary, but you can probably find a way to bring your own a few times a week and bank the difference.

Come to terms with your weaknesses. What is your weakness? Everyone has at least one. Are you an impulse buyer who cannot resist the half off rack? Knowing how your mind works will allow you to see your vulnerabilities through fresh eyes. This knowledge can protect you from marketing ploys designed such as the strategic placement of items at the checkout count. The better you know yourself the more easily you will resist overt and covert attempts to influence you. Sticking to a budget and a shopping list will also help.

Stop over-saving. Paying off high interest loans is more important than packing a low interest bank account or low yield mutual fund. A surprising number of people have money in none interest baring accounts while they carry a balance on their credit cards. It is understandable and important to have an emergency reserve. However, you would be better served to have a zero balance on your credit card. The point not that you should save less, but rather that if you are tripping over draft fees, racking up credit card balances and going financing your lifestyle with yet unearned future income you need to re-evaluate. Cut back wherever possible first, and then look at how much money you are setting aside in savings and what those funds are yielding. If your savings is not earning enough to cover the over-draft fees it might be wise to cut back in this area temporarily.

Stop carrying debt. Credit cards, student loans, car loans, and mortgages can be silent wealth thieves. If you are carrying down a $10,000 credit balance with a 15 percent interest rate, you are paying $100 a month in interest for the privilege. If you are paying off a $10,000 car loan at 6 percent, then you are wasting $50 a month on more interest.

5 Tips to End Living Paycheck to Paycheck

The lack of money has always been a perennial problem for individuals and families of all ages. In tough economic times, this difficulty evolves into a major challenge. Many individuals live their whole lives paycheck to paycheck, unable to enjoy vacations, fun purchases, or comfortable homes without incurring a mountain of debt that seems more and more unlikely to ever go away. How is it possible to escape this spiral of debt? Here are five tips of debt management and refocusing priorities to help you escape the debt spiral and break out of the "paycheck to paycheck" cycle.

1) Cut back on unplanned spending. While one of the goals of breaking out of the debt cycle is the ability to enjoy unplanned spending-like eating out or going to movies-to break out of the cycle in the first place, you need to sacrifice. For one month, track every purchase you make. At the end of the month, critically analyze your actions. Did you really need to eat out all those times, or buy that item you saw on sale in the store? By cutting out unnecessary purchases you can save a substantial amount of money each month.

2) Create a monthly budget. Now that you have your monthly purchases tracked, design a budget that takes into account your needs, but shaves off the unnecessary spending you discovered earlier.

3) Get a part-time job. If you are already working a full schedule, congratulations! You are well on your way to independence from debt. However, one of the best moves for any individual to make is to look for a part-time job to expand your income. Even if it is just a few hours a week, that provides additional income to help get your debt under control.

4) Make regular debt payments. The hardest part of paying off the debt isn't the debt itself, but the interest that accumulates each month. The only way to get the interest under control is to make regular, scheduled payments for as large of an amount as your budget allows. While credit card companies do allow you to make minimum payments far below the amount you are spending, do not fall into that trap. Always pay off credits cards in their entirety if you can, and that will begin to help you out of the debt whole.

5) Craft a five-year plan. Where do you want to be in five years? The best way to inspire yourself to get out of debt is to see where you are going. The sky is the limit, and with a firm plan, you can give yourself the confidence to escape that spiral. The road out of debt is a long and treacherous one, and it requires patience and self-sacrifice, but the eventual rewards are definitely worth the effort.

Chapter V

10 Ways to Save Money to Buy a House If You Are Living Paycheck to Paycheck

CareerBuilder.com reports that nearly 50% of us live paycheck to paycheck just to make ends meet. You know you should be putting some money into savings to buy a house, but it's hard to do when you're struggling to pay for necessities. In fact, 25% of us don't save at all. Of the people that do, over a third of them save less than $100 per month. And it's not just lower paid workers who are struggling. A quarter of the people surveyed make more than $100,000 per year. Surely there is some room for cutting back in order to one day buy a house. Here are 15 ways to make sure you have money to save each month.

1) Make a budget and a pact. Put your savings goals in writing and then make a promise to yourself or your partner that you will put money into savings to buy a house, no matter what.

2) Adjust your withholding - If you got a tax refund this year, you may be taking too many deductions. Talk with your benefits coordinator to reduce your deductions and increase your take home pay. Then earmark that extra money you are not used to seeing for savings to buy a house.

3) Don't spend this year's extra paychecks - If you are paid every other week, you will get 3 paychecks a month twice this year. Put those extra week's worth of pay in savings to buy a house.

4) Breakup with your cell phone company - If you can do it without too much penalty, break your contract and get pay as you go cell phones that are cheaper. If you can't get out of your contract, check out Cellswapper.com or CellTradeUSA.com to see if they will buy your contract.

5) Adjust your utilities - Not only can you save money to buy a house by lowering (or raising) your thermostat a couple degrees and turning it off when you are not at home, if you're in an area where there are competing utilities or aggregates, check out the options.

6) Cable/Internet - Cable television is not a necessity! Pay for basic cable. Check out movies for free at the library. Call your provider and see if you can get a better deal rather than cancel. Then bank that money you have been used to spending.

7) Swap your car - Find a car that meets your basic requirements to lower your car payments. Or look into leasing.

8) Break your addictions - Cigarettes are expensive. So is beer. Think of how much you could save if you put the money you normally spend on these items into savings to buy a house.

9) Stop eating out - The drive through coffee can easily be replaced by home brew and a stainless steel to go mug. Wait until you get home rather than stopping for a smoothie after gym. Pack your lunch. Eat leftovers.

10) Reduce your travel expenses - If you have options for public transportation, take them. Or see if you can work from home, even one day a week. And of course, there is always the carpooling option.

With just a few adjustments to your lifestyle, you can start to save money to buy a house.

Invest in Real Estate!

We work hard for our money, yet for a lot of us we continue to struggle just to make ends meet. Most of us are in debt in one form or another, debt like a home mortgage, car loans and credit card debt. The cost of living has also gone up, yet it seems our wages earned remain stagnant. Even with wage increases we find that it is not proportional to the cost increases we see in today's world. We see are basic needs such as food and gas sky rocket in cost. Parents find it harder to pay for their kid's college education. Even with medical insurance provided by our employers we still see premium increases that are deducted from our payroll check, and in some cases some benefit packages do not have all the necessary coverage our family needs, causing some people to pay out of pocket expenses for additional coverage.

Recently with the stock market decline we've seen in 2008 and continuing in 2009, the result as we have heard from so many people! Loss of entire investment funds that have devastated their hopes of retirement and or other investments people have made for their future. For most of us, we live pay check to pay check! And if for some reason that paycheck no longer comes in, how are we going to cover our debts and living expenses! Even with a two income family when one stops receiving income it could still have a negative impact on the family's finances. Loss of income for only one income earner in the family can be very serious, we are so dependent on that pay check for survival!

There is good news, there is a better way! You can, if you change the way in which you secure your financial future. Still one of the most effective ways is through real estate, even in today's market! Many experts say this is a perfect time to invest, with the drop in homes prices and interest rates still very low, the opportunities are endless! A lot of investors are making millions during this down turn in the real estate market. Most of these experts also say no matter what climate the market is in they continue to make profits in investing. There is no magic wand we can wave to be successful in the real estate market. First we need to obtain information and gain knowledge on how to make profitable investments. A friend once told me knowledge is the secret to success. Of course gaining this knowledge is a big part of this equation, however nothing will be accomplished if it does not turn into action! What good is knowledge if you do not use it to get your goals and dreams realized!

Another important bit of advice is have more than one technique for investing this will increase your chances of success, a friend of mine was very fortunate to have a mentor that was an expert in the real estate market. This mentor took him under his wing and taught him winning strategies that he applied and used out in the real estate market, which in turn has made him a lot of money! He no longer works a nine to five job, through his real estate investments he has generated a positive cash flow every month in excess of 8,000 dollars a month, all this he accomplished through investing in less than a year! He now has achieved financial freedom and continues to invest. He told me it has changed his entire life. Living pay check to pay check is now a thing of the past.

Reality Check For Those Living Paycheck to Paycheck

If you are living paycheck to paycheck, the cycle can seem like it is never going to end. Before you know it, life seems like a downward spiral of never having enough and barely getting by. You are trying to not only keep food on the table, but also prevent foreclosure on your home and all those annoying phone calls from creditors and bill collectors. Well, it is time to have a reality check and get off the living paycheck to paycheck train. By applying these tips, financial freedom is a possibility.

Pay yourself first

One secret to financial freedom is to pay yourself first. "Well how can I do that if there is not ever enough money by the end of the month?" You may ask. Pay yourself first always. When a bill collector is calling and pressuring you for their money, you will find a way to pay them, but you will never put that kind of pressure on yourself. Whether it is $10.00 or $100.00 a month, just start somewhere and start now. The sooner you start, the more you'll save and the quicker you will be to no longer living paycheck to paycheck.

Analyze your needs and your wants

So many people say there is just no way to cut any of their monthly expenses. However they keep spending on things that are not absolute necessities. In today's society the lines between needs and wants have become more blurred than ever before.

If you can not make ends meet consider if you have spent money on any of these items:

- Cable Television
- Text messaging
- Dinner out
- Salon services like manicures, pedicures and massages
- Gym memberships
- Vacations
- Electronic gadgets

All of these things are wants not needs. Consider eliminating just a few of these things and you will start seeing a difference almost instantly in your monthly budget.

Start your emergency fund

A rainy day is bound to come, your tires are going to need replacing and your kids are probably going to get sick. Do not be surprised when those things happen, be prepared. Have foresight to be ready for when life throws you a curve ball.

Start now, by paying yourself first, analyzing your needs and wants and building your emergency fund. By doing these three things you will not only stop living from paycheck to paycheck, but you will feel empowered in the process.

We provide Borrowers nationwide with a service geared to make the loan process as stress-free and simple as possible. Our Lenders and brokers across the country are given accounts to access borrower information and make successful loans.

Chapter VI

It is Time For a Change - Financial Freedom is Not Just a Dream

At a certain point in life, many people resign themselves into accepting the fact that they will never achieve the financial freedom that they thought was possible earlier in their lives. Oftentimes, as time goes by, many of the dreams of youth start to dwindle away. With the onset of adulthood and the responsibilities of having a family, getting a paycheck becomes the main priority. For quite a few people, liking what they do is not a luxury they can afford. It is simply a necessity. While it frequently appears that other people are living the lives that they dreamed of living rather than they themselves, the brass ring that once seemed so within reach, has now faded into the distance. There is still a way, however, that anyone, regardless of their current financial, psychological or family circumstances, can change things around and get back in the game. If you are living paycheck-to-paycheck, hardly able to afford anything that is outside of your budget, no need to worry. There are opportunities to start your own business with very little if any investment costs, and you can begin by working part time right from the comfort of your own home.

The home based business industry is booming, but not all home businesses are alike, of course. One of the most profitable industries today is what is commonly referred to as the network marketing industry. Now, while many people are familiar with this form of business, few really take the time to research what it is all about. Some dismiss the idea out of hand due to what they have heard form other people or from popular myth. Network marketing has evolved. Nowadays, a person can start a business with a product they never see, never ship, or exchange money for.

Everything is done online. Of course, you will see your own product in the fridge or cupboard, but the internet has changed the way this business is built forever. A person, sitting in the comfort of his or her own living room can now create a business worldwide. This was not even possible just a few short years ago. Check out network marketing companies online. They offer free training and support, a free website, access to distribution centers located worldwide, in demand product lines, and lucrative compensation plans that can eventually become a 7 figure income. Believe in yourself. You don't have to resign yourself to a paycheck-to-paycheck existence anymore.

Chapter VII

Paycheck to Paycheck Paramedic Method

A lot of us have been there before. We go through some tough financial times, we start getting deeper and deeper into debt to compensate, and every month we're further and further behind. You have to make the decision behind which bill to pay, which to put off, which to ignore completely until the collectors start to call. Often we blame circumstances or the state of the world's financial environment for this destructive habit, but what it comes down to is living from paycheck to paycheck is a personal problem that we create for ourselves. Bad financial habits will kill you no matter how many tempting credit card offers are thrown at you, no matter what's going on in the economy at large.

Thankfully, just as it's in your power to get yourself into a bad financial situation, it's also within your power to pull yourself out of one- though it's a lot more difficult. Here are a few steps that will help reverse the worst habits and get you back on solid ground.

First, you want to stop accruing liabilities. Most of our financial liabilities come through either subscription services that nickel and dime us, or through debt payments. Canceling all but the absolutely necessary subscription services will go a long way to freeing up some spare cash every month. Most of us don't use these services to the point where they become worthwhile, so it's best to simply avoid them. Another good thing to avoid is going further into debt. It's crucial that you stop using your credit cards or other methods of accruing debt if you're going to get into a strong financial position. Get out of the liabilities you are able to escape, and stop accruing more.

After minimizing liabilities, it's a good idea to start saving money. At first it doesn't matter just how much you are saving, it just matters that you are saving something, so you get into the habit of living on less than you earn, while thinking ahead towards the future. While it's important to save at least a little bit out of each paycheck to keep your savings growing over time, it's also important to save more aggressively at first to ensure you have a good emergency fund in place. Most financial experts recommend having a buffer of around $1000 to start, though this will depend upon your income and expenses.

Once you've reduced liabilities and begun to save, it's time to make sure you start spending consciously. It's a good idea to track your spending regularly so you know exactly where your money goes. By reviewing this data once a month and figuring out which of your expenditures are worthwhile and which aren't is a great way to start eliminating the spending that just isn't worth it. By doing so, you free up money to allocate to those areas of your life that will pay dividends- whether its savings, investing, debt reduction, or simply those luxuries that really make you happy.

Chapter VIII

12 Secrets To Reduce Your Debt And Stop Living From Paycheck To Paycheck

Eighty percent of Americans are broke before their next paycheck is deposited in the bank! Easy credit and large credit limits from credit card companies has allowed Americans to purchase a life of stress, anxiety and guilt. Of course, this is only half of the equation. The other half is...

Overspending. The age-old and foolish tradition of keeping up with the Jones is being replaced with a greater foolishness - keeping ahead of the Jones. Some people must have the very best of everything or some simply must have "everything".

These unrestrained desires lead to a condition called oniomania. People that suffer from oniomania are referred to as "shop-aholics". Shopping and spending money temporarily suspends negative feelings the shop-aholic is having. The long-term consequences of unbearable debt, guilt and stress are never brought to mind until it is too late.

This overspending also leads to an out-of-control clutter condition. Closets overflow into living spaces. Living spaces fill-up until the home is no longer a calm and inviting place. This leads to a vicious circle. The additional stress and anxiety caused by a cluttered and dirty home leads to more shopping to relieve the anxiety and stress.

Symptoms: Like all addictions, oniomania, has common symptoms:

- Shopping or spending money because of being disappointed, angry or scared
- Shopping/spending habits are causing emotional distress or chaos in your life

- Getting into arguments with others about your shopping/spending
- Feeling lost without your credit cards
- Buying items with credit cards that you probably would not buy with cash
- When dining out with friends or business associates, you almost always insist on picking up the tab-- whether you can actually afford to, or not
- Spending money causes a "rush" and anxiety at the same time
- Shopping and spending money feels like you are doing something forbidden or reckless in your otherwise careful life
- Feeling guilty, ashamed, embarrassed or confused after shopping or spending money
- Many purchases are never used. The price tag/sticker is still attached.

- Lying to others about what you bought or how much you spent
- Thinking about money - how much I have, how much I owe, how much I want to have
- Spending a lot of time juggling accounts and bills to accommodate spending

The one symptom that all addictions share is industrial strength denial. In order to overcome the denial a brutal self-assessment of their behavior and the reasons underlying those feelings is required.

Twelve things to do to reduce your debt and have money left at the end of the week:

- Do not carry credit cards/checkbooks around with you.
- Make a shopping list and only buy what is on the list.
- Keep only a limited amount of cash on you - for essentials.

- Destroy all credit cards except for one for emergency use only
- Don't window shop - 'lead us not into temptation!' Or, only after the store is closed.

Avoid discount warehouses and big box stores. Have a certain amount of cash to spend if you do go to one. Many big box stores include groceries. It's hard to avoid going since we need to eat. Do this: Write-out your grocery list and do NOT deviate from the list. Do NOT wander into the general merchandise areas of the store.

Stay away from catalogs, TV Shopping Channels and Internet stores.

Don't play games or try to justify purchases.

Try to avoid advertisements (magazines, newspapers, fliers, etc.), where possible.

Plan other activities when you would normally go recreational shopping. Take a walk, do some gardening or exercise, call a friend and chat.

Talk it over with someone else. The "Buddy System" works for compulsive spenders the same as it does for other addictions.

Start a blog. When you feel the urge to shop/spend, start blogging about how you are feeling. Include those feelings of regret, anxiety and depression that come after the shopping spree. There are free internet blogging sites and you can use an anonymous screen/web name. Nobody ever needs to know who you are if you want to keep your identity a secret.

Earn a Second Income From Home

If you are counting down the time until you get your next paycheck you are not alone. Many people are finding themselves living paycheck to paycheck. And they are doing this with only the hope of making ends meet.

We have all been told to put a certain percentage of our wages aside, prepare for hard times and emergencies. While this is good advice, it is impossible to achieve when you are living paycheck to paycheck. Everything we hear on the economy is telling us things will only get worse before they get better. How much worse can it get?

We are told to set a budget. Okay, good advice. We do this and still find that we are living paycheck to paycheck. A budget provides for the rent or house payment, the monthly utility bills, and groceries. There is even an amount factored in for the occasional dinner out, buying new tires, and money spent for fun.

What is not factored in is that everything but the paycheck is going up. Working forty hours plus and still no extra money. It is hard to stretch one paycheck far enough to be able to live a regular, everyday life. And harder still to put back any cash for the future.

In this economic climate, we are struggling just to meet the necessary expenses. Living paycheck to paycheck is not going to pay off the mortgage, put the kids through college, or provide us with a comfortable retirement. To have money left over at the end of the month just seems to be out of the question.

Sometimes, though living paycheck to paycheck, it is not just a matter of where the money went or how it was spent. It is simply a case of basic math - you may not be earning enough to ever get ahead. A decision must be made as to whether or not you are happy with the way things are, or do you need to earn more?

There are various ways a person could earn a second income; another job working for someone else, or work for yourself. And there are both pros and cons to either working for yourself or having a boss.

A second job, outside of the home, while a good option, requires even more time away from the family. You are answering to someone else and having to get permission to take time off. While it may alleviate some of the worries brought on by living paycheck to paycheck, it is not your only solution.

Even though our economy is in a recession it is actually a good time to begin a new business and earn second income from home. All you need do is research on the internet to realize the numerous opportunities that are there. Google the phrase "make money online" and you will see what I am talking about.

There is no right way or wrong way to go about achieving success in a work at home business. You will discover multiple strategies that are being utilized by people today. And the best part about many of these techniques is that they are either free or require a minimal amount of start-up capital. So even though you are working paycheck to paycheck it is very possible for you to earn second income from home.

Saving for Retirement - A Challenge for Paycheck to Paycheck Employees

Allow me, if you will, to offer the following definition of retirement. Retirement is the state of having separated from one's paycheck-to-paycheck job. The "paycheck-to-paycheck" description is important. The majority of people who retire to incomes lower than their pre-retirement levels are paycheck-to-paycheck employees. Chances are, since you're reading this article, you're one of the paycheck-to-paycheck people.

Let's say this is you: You've got a decent job, maybe a good one. Most of your paycheck is being eaten up by life's necessities, but you manage to put away as much as you can into your 401(k) retirement plan. Retirement is looming in the not-too-distant future, and the prospect for accumulating enough savings or investments that will equal your present income by retirement age seems very bleak indeed. Still, you get serious about saving for retirement. You might even engage the services of a Certified Financial Planner. Part of your plan is based on maximizing Social Security benefits. Now what?

Financial planners rarely, if ever, plan for you, the client- retiree to retire financially independent (with the exception of the few high income clients). What most financial planners don't tell you is they target a 20-35% decrease of income to you in retirement. The decrease may be as high as 50%! That's not a knock on financial planning or financial planners. Most of them are doing the best they can with what they have to work with. There generally is simply too much month at the end of each paycheck for most people.

Herein is the age-old problem: Most people in the United States of America, I repeat, do not earn enough money to live comfortably during their pre-retirement years and retire comfortably as well. That means any financial planning you do is being done to target a decrease in your living standards by 20 to 50 % in retirement!

Remember, you do not have to live on less in retirement. No matter where you are right now financially, you can build and enjoy a retirement lifestyle you desire. Peace.

Chapter IX

60% of Americans Living Paycheck to Paycheck

The economy in the U. S. is bad, and though they keep trying to tell us that it's getting better, we haven't even begun to see the inflation that's inevitable because of all the big bailouts the government just printed wads of cash to cover. So, what will happen to people when their paychecks no longer cover their expenses? What will happen when they can no longer afford the little perks that we've all come to love... like a Starbucks latte in the morning?

Here's where Internet marketing is a great fit. You don't have to put all of your energy into a mega business, earning millions of dollars a year like the big gurus. But how would it feel to make a couple of thousand dollars a month extra? Imagine what you could do with just that much. Buy a new car. Take vacations. Or pay your kid's college tuition without needing to take out loans. How cool would that be?

Well... It's totally possible. All you need is a little capital (less than $100 a month) and a system to follow. When you have a proven system that works, you shouldn't even consider whether you might be able to get cheaper online services than what the system recommends, or how you can tweak the system to your personal preference. You just do it!

Proven systems work like recipes. If you substitute peanut butter for cherries, your recipe will come out all wrong. And if you tweak the recipe to make it more healthy, by using one less egg, your efforts may well go right into the garbage. That just doesn't work! You need to follow the system blindly, without asking questions or changing any of its steps. If it has worked for others, it will work for you, too.

Do a little poking around. See what people are saying about systems you find. Have real people made money with it? How many are satisfied customers? Does the person or company involved resonate with your personal sensibilities? Figuring this out will take a little time, but it's really best not to jump into the first thing that comes along.

And stay far, far away from Internet marketing programs that tell you that you can make money while you sleep, that you can do it for free, and that you don't have to do any work. They lie. You need to work on your system, or you need to find qualified people to build it for you. And you can't make money without some investment of your own. Granted, start up will cost you far less than an offline business, but it will still take some investment. If you think you can't afford it, understand this: You can't afford not to.

Paycheck Stubs - The Essentials of Making One

There are a number of things that you need to be aware of when it comes to making paycheck stubs. A stub is required by employees in order to show proof of income. In other words, it is also used to understand the terms of payment over a given period of time.

It is important to point out that companies have different approaches when it comes to calculating paycheck stubs. Some make use of software which allows them to quickly generate checks which they can easily print later on. However now all of this can be done on the internet. You will be able to find some websites that allow you to do this for free whereas others may charge you a certain fee for their services.

Paycheck stubs are commonly referred to as paycheck slips. However, you will find some websites promoting them as wage statements and pay advice. In most states the employers are bounded by law to provide their employees with detailed information regarding the calculation of their income and the terms of payments. The eventual itemized statement will provide a detailed information regarding the applicable deductions and the actual earnings of the employee. Furthermore, it should have the specific pay period dates such as biweekly or monthly.

Paycheck stubs typically reflect the regular working hours of the employee and the regular pay rate along with the gross pay rate. At the same time, they will mention any overtime hours along with the overtime pay rates. Benefit days like sick leaves, vacations, holidays, personal time will also be mentioned and the amounts that are related with these as well.

When looking to make a paycheck stub it is important to be aware of the essentials so that you do not go wrong irrespective of the tools you will be using.

Chapter X

Paycheck Advances Online: A Much Needed Service

Paycheck advance loans are always in the news. If there isn't a new regulation being proposed, a tale of a customer's finances gone awry or a company sued in the courts writers will still find something to talk about when it comes to short-term paycheck advances online. How do you view the business? The opposition looks at the service as businesses looking to take advantage of low income customers. Those who are for the payday loan service appreciate the option; it gives the freedom of choice. When there is no place left to get money help, wouldn't you want some door to open?

Once upon a time, there were unregulated private lenders, also known as loan sharks who provided high interest loans to those in need. Nowadays, companies provide short-term loans based on qualifications. These businesses evolved from loan shark opportunities to safe paycheck loans online through lots of trial, error and regulations. The demand is there. Customers want the option; they need alternative methods to help solve small money problems.

Banks and credit unions joined the paycheck advance business providing customers their own version of a short-term loan. The idea was to provide access to fast cash to those who had active accounts. Many people liked these loan options since it cut out the research of finding a safe payday lender from the bunch of lenders. There were successful loans processed, but there were also failures. The banks' customers were finding similar problems to those with failed payday loan companies. The payoff was still a burden to those living paycheck to paycheck. In recent news, three of the larger banks are now pulling out of the short-term loan business. They will no longer offer this type of service to customers. Why? It wasn't because there was a lack of business.

It seems that customers who use a bank's services still had trouble repaying the loans. There was a cycle of debt, large payments, high interest and the banks were able to control a customer's account. There may have been fewer fees since loan extension was not an option, but they collected more on repeat loans. Banks takes payment directly out of the accounts and the customer is left in a hole. They take out a new loan to survive the next pay period and then hit the same wall a few short weeks later. Regulatory committees investigate when customers cry foul. It doesn't change the fact that some sort of paycheck advance is in demand. People need more money management education. These loans work for those who make the payment a priority. It also helps to use a safe payday loan company that offers payment options. Borrowers may not be able to afford the full payoff, but at least they can pay it down and lower fees. Obtaining a new loan creates large fees all over again.

People need time to work money problems out. Time is money and when it comes to the lending industry, time is translated into finance charges. The option to apply is there, it is not a mandatory service.

Now the postal service is working on getting into the industry. Not only will their service provide their version of a payday loan, 'postal loan', but it will help those people without bank accounts limit paycheck cashing fees. Check cashing is a service that comes with a fee. People spend money to get access to their own money. The USPS will place your direct deposited paycheck onto a card for customers to use. If they need a loan, the postal service will offer up to 50% of the deposited amount. The fees are much smaller, but half your paycheck is a big chunk to pay back. Safe paycheck advance lenders would never loan that much of a person's take home pay. The USPS will have access to your paycheck to collect full payment if the customer falls behind. What position will this put the customer back in? It seems like the post office will experience similar results as the banks. Eventually, people will fall into a cycle of debt here too.

Research your options and make the best choices for your personal situation. Don't assume that one offer is better than the other as each business is out to make money in addition to providing a service in demand. Look at prices and payment options and find something that will fit into your budget.

Conclusion

Lately, I've been hearing so much about how baby boomers can't afford to retire, how people are buried in debt, the struggles families are having just making ends meet and so on and so on.

The real problem here, the big thing stopping most people is that they believe there's nothing they can do about it.

They bought (no pun intended) into the idea that their paycheck is all they have to play with. I use the word play here because the more you begin to see money as a game, one which you can win, the better off you'll be.

www.ingramcontent.com/pod-product-compliance
Lightning Source LLC
Chambersburg PA
CBHW070302220526
45465CB00004B/1717